HOW TO TALK TO ANYONE AND EVERYBODY

Step By Step Instructions To Converse With Individuals

By

Richard C. Cervantez

Copyright © 2022 Richard C. Cervantez

TABLE OF CONTENTS

INTRODUCTION

There's a workmanship to bantering with others.

It's adequately not to know how to capably initiate a discussion with somebody - you

must have the option to keep the individual locked in, add intriguing data, and in any case

keep away from terrible conversational propensities.

While certain individuals are naturals, others could absolutely benefit from some assistance.

That is the reason we set up this helpful aide

on the most proficient method to converse with anybody, about anything.

The accompanying tips will assist you with exploring discussions - whether you're at an espresso shop, a mixed drink party or a gathering room.

CHAPTER ONE
Present Yourself

This won't work in each setting, yet entirely in numerous cases, old fashioned "Hello there!

I'm this and that; Thought I'd present myself!" will get the job done.

As amazing as this sounds, individuals feel more extraordinary assuming you approach them and present yourself.

It goes for guts to stroll up to somebody and be the first to talk.

The way that you made a special effort to do this, will cause the individual to feel significant

- what's more, will likely make them need to talk as far as you might be concerned, also.

CHAPTER TWO
Request Help

You don't must have an extraordinary opening line to begin conversing with somebody.

You can begin by requesting some assistance.

It tends to be a truly valuable discussion, as a matter of fact starter - obviously, it must be in setting.

For instance, on the off potential for success that you're having at a transport
stop, you can say: "Excuse me, do you know how frequently the transport runs?"

Regardless of whether you definitely know the solution to the question, this approach can be an extraordinary way to begin a discussion with somebody - on the grounds that a great many people like to feel supportive.

CHAPTER THREE
Request Their Viewpoint

Each individual has their own perspective on the world- so take that for your own potential benefit, and begin getting some information about their viewpoints:

For instance:
"What is your take of this spot?"
"What's your number one mix of espresso?"

Stay with lighter subjects from the start, such as your environmental elements, food, beverages, or music- this ought to give you motivation to begin a fast, yet intriguing discussion.

In the event that the individual is available to chatting with you, you can ring in with your own perspectives - to move the discussion along.

CHAPTER FOUR
Reference A Subject That Has Common Claim

Another helpful methodology, is to make reference to something that had recently happened.

For example, in the event that you were going to a discussion, you could ignite up a discussion with somebodywho was likewise in a similar meeting.

It makes it simpler to reference a particular theme.

Suppose that you were going to a Tony Robbins occasion.

You definitely know that every other person joining in the occasion honestly loves his.

In this way, you could ask what their #1 books are, or on the other hand on the off chance that they saw his Netflix unique.

The point is to attempt to keep the subject you reference, somewhat unambiguous.

By restricting yourself to something explicit, you can really open up much more entryways for natural discussion.

CHAPTER FIVE
Utilize Inconspicuous Humor

Utilizing humor is one more incredible method for beginning conversing with somebody, when proper - you

likely don't have any desire to attempt this at a memorial service…

The stunt here is to involve humor as a device, furthermore, not make jokes to the detriment of others.

You need to get individuals giggling with you, furthermore, abstain from appearing to be inconsiderate or annoying in any capacity.

Ensure that your humor is connected with the discussion or the event.

In the event that you have a practiced story, sit tight for the perfect opportunity to say it.

CHAPTER SIX
Keep Steady Over The News

Being know all about recent developments is totally the most ideal way to have an adequate number of subjects to bring up in any discussion.

The subjects don't need to be weighty, or include inside and out skill.

Just, attempt to leave the climate outside…

Since, except if you're a meteorologist,
the possibilities that you or any other person has something

genuinely fascinating to say regarding the climate is tiny.

CHAPTER SEVEN
Pose Unconditional Inquiries

Individuals for the most part prefer to discuss themselves.

Not dependably on the grounds that they're narcissistic, in any case, frequently in light of the fact that it's a protected subject, and one they clearly know well overall.

In the event that you're battling to consider what to say, just pose great inquiries.

Posing inquiries shows a degree of individual interest and makes the other individual feel really focused on.

So how would you track down the right inquiries to inquire?

By basically focusing and cautiously noticing the individual, to track down pieces of information.

For instance, in the event that they have a decent hairdo, you can say: "Your hair looks perfect.

What hair items do you utilize?"

The key is to pose unconditional inquiries and make them talk - as opposed to seeking clarification on some pressing issues that evoke yes or no responses.

This permits the individual to expand more, furthermore, it makes all the difference for the discussion - it moreover assists you with figuring out more about their character.

CHAPTER EIGHT
Go For Praises

Very much like individuals like to hear themselves talk,
they love it considerably more when another person has pleasant comments.

Praising individuals is an extraordinary method for getting a discussion going, and it's likewise an incredible method for staying to somebody.

By praising somebody on something explicit - like their grin, their gems or their shoes - you increment your possibilities being recalled and popular.

CHAPTER NINE
Reword What They Say

Some of the time, discussions can wind down in the event that you can't truly connect with the subject being discussed.

In the event that you have little information regarding the matter, it very well may be difficult to add your viewpoint - and off-kilterquiets can follow.

For this situation, a decent method, is to reword what the other individual has said.

Assuming that somebody is portraying their convoluted occupation to you or a calling you're not comfortable with, they might be very much aware of your needof information.

By rehashing what they say or requesting explanation, you're making a feeling of interest and compatibility.

Not in the least does this show that you're tuning in to what they're talking about, yet it gives them an opportunity to bring up errors - and your advantage makes them anxious to tell you more.

CHAPTER TEN
Offer Little Things About Yourself

Certain individuals track down sharing things about themselves unnatural - and this is particularly valid for thoughtful people.

Be that as it may, sharing little things - regardless how unimportant - will show the other individual that YOU Believe they should get to know you.

The thought is to positive about raise
points, and not to overthink how you come across with your words.

It's truly not about what's being said
in a discussion that individuals recollect the most - they recollect how they felt in your presence.

CHAPTER ELEVEN
Recount Your Story

At times, individuals answer quicker in the event that you tell them a little bit about yourself previously you request their story.

Consider a story that intently interfaces with the ongoing circumstance you're in, and just share it.

For instance: "I hung tight for five hours at the air terminal a day or two ago.

I trust this flight will be on time today."

Assuming that you're straightforward with your words and sentiments, the other individual will open dependent upon you and jump in on the discussion.

CHAPTER TWELVE
Stay Positive And Keep An Open Mind

Have you at any point met somebody who recently grumbled about everything?

It's irritating right?

On the other side, somebody who stays positive, furthermore, shows a real and open point of view toward

their environmental elements, appears to draw normally individuals in.

Obviously, it is more straightforward said to remain positive than done.

Having the option to keep an uplifting perspective requires some pondering.

You really want to pursue being extremely mindful, what's more, screen the way that you respond to different circumstances.

At the point when you end up inclining toward pessimism in the manner you impart, attempt to address the way of behaving.

In time, you will discover yourself feeling more sure - and therefore, really enchanting to everyone around you.

CHAPTER THIRTEEN
Don't Keep Down Your Energy

Your most memorable tendency might be to stifle your energy and excitement, hold your hands

in your pockets when you need to signal, what's more, by and large stay 'cool'.

Nonetheless, individuals will ordinarily respond more decidedly when you show excitement through

hand signals, looks, and you talk with various tones and volumes.

This makes a discussion seriously intriguing - what's more, we would all prefer associate with somebody

fun and vivacious, than somebody dull and
dormant.

CHAPTER FOURTEEN
Don't Accept Individuals Will Concur With You

Research on friendly brain science shows that numerous of us take part in the "accepted closeness predisposition."

It's undependable to reason that for no obvious reason you are against an ideological group, that the individual you're conversing with is, also.

However, discussions can make for pleasant discussions.

On the off chance that you simply expect that everybody thinks and feels the manner in which you do, it's probably you'll get gotten off to a bad start - and end up with it in your mouth.

CHAPTER FIFTEEN
Know When Not To Talk

At times quietness can feel off-kilter.

Your normal tendency might be to fill that quietness with chatter.

Notwithstanding, there are times that it is ideal to keep quiet.

On the off chance that you're exhausted on a plane, you may need to engage yourself by conversing with the individual sitting close to you.

Yet, assuming they are giving you clear friendly prompts flagging that they are not intrigued in conversing with you, you ought to see as another method for entertaining yourself.

Assuming somebody is staying away from eye to eye connection, that is
a sign that they don't want to talk.

Somebody who is perusing or paying attention to earphones
is likely likewise happy to stay quiet.

Conversing with outsiders CAN threaten,
yet, it doesn't Need to be.

Set yourself up with these techniques for beginning a discussion, and you'll be fine.

Sooner or later, you might try and disregard how abnormal you felt from the beginning.

www.ingramcontent.com/pod-product-compliance
Lightning Source LLC
Chambersburg PA
CBHW051939150726
47999CB00006B/2286